I Love Sports

Figure Skating

by Erika S. Manley

Bullfrog
Books

Ideas for Parents and Teachers

Bullfrog Books let children practice reading informational text at the earliest reading levels. Repetition, familiar words, and photo labels support early readers.

Before Reading

- Discuss the cover photo. What does it tell them?
- Look at the picture glossary together. Read and discuss the words.

Read the Book

- "Walk" through the book and look at the photos. Let the child ask questions. Point out the photo labels.
- Read the book to the child, or have him or her read independently.

After Reading

- Prompt the child to think more. Ask: Have you ever figure skated? What was your favorite part?

Bullfrog Books are published by Jump!
5357 Penn Avenue South
Minneapolis, MN 55419
www.jumplibrary.com

Library of Congress Cataloging-in-Publication Data

Names: Manley, Erika S., author.
Title: Figure skating / by Erika S. Manley.
Description: Minneapolis, MN : Jump!, Inc., [2018] | Series: I love sports | Includes index.
Audience: Age 5–8. | Audience: K to Grade 3.
Identifiers: LCCN 2017027404 (print)
LCCN 2017032382 (ebook) | ISBN 9781624966699 (ebook) | ISBN 9781620318218 (hardcover : alk. paper) | Subjects: LCSH: Figure skating—Juvenile literature. | Classification: LCC GV850.4 (ebook)
LCC GV850.4 .M35 2018 (print) | DDC 796.91/2—dc23
LC record available at https://lccn.loc.gov/2017027404

Editor: Jenna Trnka
Book Designer: Leah Sanders
Photo Researcher: Leah Sanders

Photo Credits: Roman Samokhin/Adobe Stock, cover; Dmitry Morgan/Shutterstock, 1; Yasonya/Shutterstock, 3; Westend61/SuperStock, 4, 23bl; arinahabich/iStock, 5; Thomas Barwick/Getty, 6–7; Danielle Earl Photography, 8–9, 14, 15, 22bl; Vladimir Vasiltvich/Shutterstock, 10, 11, 16–17, 20–21, 22tl, 22tr, 22br, 23tl; StockphotoVideo/Shutterstock, 18–19, 23tr; vnlit/Shutterstock, 23br; Khakimullin Aleksandr/Shutterstock, 24.

Printed in the United States of America at Corporate Graphics in North Mankato, Minnesota.

Table of Contents

Let's Figure Skate!

Grab your skates.
Lace them up tight.

Let's skate!

rink

We go to the rink.

Ann steps on the ice.

Woah!

It is slippery.

Finn uses his blades.

He pushes against
the ice.

It moves him forward.

He glides.

blade

Cam skates fast.

She does a spiral.
One foot stays
in the air.

Look!
Ali spins.
She spins fast!

Ria uses her toe pick.

She pushes off the ice.

toe pick

14

She jumps!

15

Ana does crossovers.

One foot goes over the other.

Today is the ice show!

It is time to show our skills.

We skate our routine.

Do you want to skate?

Grab your skates!

Let's go!

Figure Skating Moves

crossover
A move in which one foot steps over the other while skating. This move helps you skate around a circle or curve.

spin
Figure skaters can spin on one skate or two. The arms and legs are held in tight.

jump
A move in which the figure skater leaves the ice. Toe picks help the skater push off and jump into the air.

spiral
A move in which the figure skater glides on one foot while raising the other leg above hip level.

Picture Glossary

ice show
A show where figure skaters perform routines for an audience.

routine
A performance that is practiced.

lace
To tie by drawing laces through holes.

toe pick
The saw-like part on the front of the blade that helps skaters stop and jump.

Index

To Learn More

Learning more is as easy as 1, 2, 3.

1) Go to www.factsurfer.com

2) Enter "figureskating" into the search box.

3) Click the "Surf" button to see a list of websites.

With factsurfer.com, finding more information is just a click away.